HOT PROFITS WITH SUBLIMATION

Increasing Your Sales With SUBLIMATION

By Timothy M. Braun

Sublimation is the transition of a substance directly from the solid phase to the gas phase without passing through an intermediate liquid phase. (Wikipedia)

You don't have to be a brain surgeon to start a sublimation business. It's not easy, but it's not hard… it just takes a lot of work and a commitment to be in business for yourself. It's fun, especially when everything comes together and you start getting orders, and some will be large, large enough to pay for all your costs and you can start making a profit.

You may not know it, but if you have a heat press, you have the ability to substantially increase your sales to your present customers and gain new customers with new promotional items. Instant T-Shirts are a great source of revenue and a great customer base builder, but why just stop at T-shirts and sweatshirts? Most customers, especially retail customers you wholesale to want merchandise that will sell. You can supply them with many different items! What about groups that constantly use promotional items to fund-raise? Do you think they only want to sell T-Shirts? The answer is "NO". They want items, just like retailers, that will sell and make them money.

What about businesses that use promotional items as sales tools? That auto dealer, insurance agent or other salesmen/saleswomen who give away mugs, keychains, etc. to keep their name in front of possible customers. That is the name of the game, making money, whether it's for you or for the groups you sell to.

Do you have a retail business and would like to add custom-made manufactured products to your line that your customers would love and need? Would you like a GREAT home business manufacturing your own products that are needed and customers love? Why sell someone else's products when you can sell your own? You can wholesale or retail for the greater profit. Advertise your products as **_Made In America!_** Most national brands can't say or do that as most are manufactured overseas. Many customers will pay a premium for anything made in America.

Would you like to be at the top? Would you like to make $$ and REALLY control your own destiny?

Whether you are a stay-at-home mom or dad, retired, handicapped or whatever, you can create a business that makes real $$ -- right from your home!

When you manufacture/make your own products you can make upwards of 90%+ profits on your products, or upwards of 600-850% ROI (Return on investment) by starting your own line of sublimated products.

They are easy to produce and we are going to show you everything, step by step! You can literally have fun; even make it a family business, and possibly turn your products into a very profitable business! There are no quotas or goals to meet. Work and learn at your own pace. There are no sales meetings you have to attend, no sales tiers to work towards. Your rewards are the goals you set and reach for yourself. You are your own boss.

If you never take that first step, nothing ever happens. Every time you resist something new, you hinder yourself from achieving anything. Fear actually stops you from going forward, and we understand that. This is an opportunity, a chance to take an opportunity, to connect with someone who has done it and use our experience to take yourself to the next level. Wherever you are today, just start! Take charge of your future!!

What do I manufacture to increase my sales? I have many different items that, for me, sell very well. There are literally hundreds of items that you can sublimate. Below are some of the items I use my heat press and mug press with. I use these two suppliers for all my sublimation products, but you can easily see all the different items that are available to you by going to their sites!
The following are from Coastal Business Supply (https://www.coastalbusiness.com/) and Conde: (http://dyetrans.com/)

Aprons
Awards
Baby
Bags
Blankets
Bookmarks
Business Card Holders
Buttons
Can Coolies
Car Flags
ChromaLuxe Photo Panels
Clipboards
Clocks
Coasters
Compact Mirrors
Cutting Boards
Desk & Door Plates
Dog Tags
Door Hangers
Doormats
Flasks
Flip Flops
Hitch Covers
iPad Cases
iPhone Cases
Jewelry

Plaques
Poker Chips
Production Jigs
Puzzles
Samsung Phone Cases
Serving Trays
Sheet Stock
Shot Glasses
Shoulder Bags
Signage
Sippy Cups
Starter Kits
Steins
Sticky Note Holders
Stockings
Subli-Patch
Sublimation Support
Tablet Cases
Tiles (Ceramic)
Tiles (Hardboard)
Tile Accessories
Tote Bags
Towels
Travel Mugs
Vapor Apparel
Water Bottles
Wide Format Sheet Stock
Wraps

Keepsake Boxes
Key Hangers
Keychains
Kindle Fire Cases
Latte Mugs
License Plates & Frames
Light Switch Covers
Lighters
Luggage & Bag Tags
Luggage Wraps
Magnets
Message Boards
Mini Basketball Goal
Mobile Device Accessories
Mousepads
Mugs
Name Badges
Neck Ties
Notebooks
Ornaments
Pet Bandanas
Pet Bowls
Pet Tags
Phone Cases
Photo Frames
Placemats

Some of the above items from the two suppliers are the same, but most are different items.

What is it going to cost you to get started in sublimation? Here's a list of a few things you will need to start your sublimation business:

1. Heat Press ($100-$400) (We discuss this below!)

2. Epson printer (preferably one that prints up to 13" x 19". (around $149.00)

3. Sublimation inks (about $50.00-$60.00)

4. Sublimation Transfer Paper ($14.00/ 100 sheets 8.5"x11")

5. Refillable cartridges for the Epson Printer (($11.99 a set)

6. High-heat tape ($6.00)

7. Adhesive spray ($5.95)

8. Mug Press (if you are going to do mugs and water bottles.) ($149.99 to $599.99)

9. Digital infrared temperature heat guns (About $35.00)

For those who don't yet own a heat press, here is what you will need.

1. Purchasing a Heat Press
You don't have to have an expensive heat press. You can purchase a great used heat press over the Internet and on E-bay. What you should look for is the top temperature of at least 400 degrees (I'll tell you why later) and a timer that will go at least 8 minutes. Look for one that has a pivoting top. It can be a clamshell type, but the top platen should be able to pivot side-to-side and front to back; not much, but it should pivot. Try not to get a clamshell that is rigid and doesn't allow for different thickness side-to-side or front to back if you can avoid it. I bought a new

pivoting head press 6 years ago for $350 and I still use it today. I also found a heat press that IS rigid on the top, but by loosening the bolds on the bottom platen, it pivots on the bottom, which is also fine.

Purchasing a Printer:

(The following printer is what I recommend as of this printing. Epson is always upgrading their printers with new models, so this one may not be always available.)

You will need another printer, as you will be using special ink we'll talk about in a few minutes. The Epson Workforce Series (WF-7610 is one of them) that I recommend for high-heat inks in my t-shirt e-book is the perfect printer for this also. It is wide-format, prints up to 13" wide and 19" long, and will use refillable cartridges. You won't need this much area for 95% of your sublimation printing, but when you need it, it's there. Besides, you can gang images easier with large sheets and save money, but most of your sublimation printing will fit on an 8.5" x 11" sheet.

If you don't want or can't afford to purchase another printer and if you have an Epson 7110 or another model that is using the high-heat inks, you can use that printer for your sublimation inks, but you will constantly have to change the cartridges and do head cleanings, which will waste a lot of ink. **Do yourself a favor, if you can afford it, purchase a separate printer.**

Digital infrared temperature heat guns

The one thing you will absolutely need is a digital infrared temperature heat gun. They only cost about $35 at Harbor Freight and will save you a tremendous amount of money and frustration. It tells you the temperature of the Heat Press just by pressing a button and aiming it at the heat platen. For the past two years, with my shirts, I had problems with the transfer not peeling right. With my signs and other items I sublimated, sometimes the ink didn't transfer all the way and the shirt, signs, or other items were ruined. Even if a small spot didn't transfer, the item was ruined, and sometimes this happened on several items in a row. I would get upset, mad, and confused, as I knew I was doing everything correctly. I didn't know if it was me, the heat press, the item, or the ink that was the problem, and you know it always happened when I was in a hurry or I had a limited number of items to work with; and it ALWAYS happened with the most expensive items!

Well, one day a while ago, someone suggested I purchase one of these digital infrared temperature heat guns, and what I found out was astonishing! My heat presses were off as much as fifty degrees from what it said it was at. It was way overheating/underheating my transfers. When I thought it was at 350 degrees, it was at 400 degrees plus!! And that, my friends, will cause any transfer to go bad. It is so hot, it actually melts the transfer film on shirts so it won't stick to the shirt and on sublimation, if it wasn't up to temperature, all the ink didn't transfer. I was clueless as to what was causing my problems, because you can't see it. But since I found this simple remedy, I haven't had one problem and haven't lost one shirt or sublimation item!

I don't know if the real expensive presses have this problem, but it will pay dividends to be sure your press is at the right temperature!

Refillable ink cartridges—

Ross (at inkjetcart.us) now carries the refillable cartridges for the Epson printers at: www.inkjetcarts.us He is very knowledgeable and will help you with any problems.

Paper-

You have to use a special paper for sublimation printing. It's not expensive. You should purchase a couple different sizes so you can be efficient in the size you use. Here is the site address for the 8.5 x 11 paper I use:

https://www.coastalbusiness.com/image-right-epson-sublimation-printing-transfer-paper-ir31-g.html

There are also several other sizes of paper available here.

Sublimation Ink—

This is where purchasing this e-book is going to pay off big for you! We do "**Small Format** Sublimation" printing. There is one company that has a patent on sublimation inks for the small format printers we use, and they are very expensive, about $259 for four 125ml bottles. However, if you do a little searching on the internet, you will find several companies that are selling sublimation ink for a very reasonable price, about 10-15% of the above price for "**large format**" sublimation printing. It took me awhile to figure it out, but here is one place you will save **BIG** from my research. The ink for the **large format** sublimation printers is the same for the **small format**! There is no reason for the high prices on some of the inks, except they have a monopoly by patent. Do your research and see for yourself. Check out PrintPayLess.com and then check out others. They say the ink is only for 42" or larger sublimation printers, but it's the same ink, and it's very inexpensive! I have been using it for years!!

High-heat tape—

This is used to tape your printed images to your mugs, signs, etc. It is relatively cheap, about $7.48 a roll as of this writing and each roll will last a very long time. Here is where I get it: https://www.coastalbusiness.com/clear-heat-resistent-tape-for-coffee-mugs-and-tiles-thermal-tape-clear-s.html

Spray adhesive—

Some companies sell a special adhesive for high heat sublimation printing, but a can of 3M from Walmart is almost as good. The 3M spray may leave a slight residue on some items, do if you don't want that, purchase the spray from Conde. Use it very sparingly, just a fine mist will do, and don't use it on the whole transfer. Just a small part will usually keep it in place.

The above items will take care of most of your sublimations. There are a few specialty items you will need if you get into porcelain plates, shot glasses or things like that.

Mousepads & Coasters—How many people and businesses use mouse pads? How many businesses use mouse pads as promotional give-a-ways? Lots. Making mouse pads and coasters are probably the easiest of all the sublimations. You can obtain coasters in foam rubber or hardboard.

Custom Clocks- Your customer will want to put photos on the face of the clocks and businesses will put their logos on them.

Ornaments (Christmas, etc.) A great profit maker! Businesses will put their logos on Christmas ornaments and small cities and towns will put their emblems on them with the year to celebrate Christmas every year.

License Plates & License Plate Frames – Again, businesses (auto dealers) will put their name and place on the frames. I've found that schools and businesses will also put their names and logos on the license plates.

Mugs Press-THE <u>REAL</u> MONEY MAKER! If you invest in sublimation, you will definitely want to purchase a mug press or two. This is perhaps the best investment as EVERYONE uses coffee mugs and I have literally sold thousands of them. I don't care who they are; businesses, schools, non-profits, individuals, etc., everyone uses them for promotions and their own use. A mug press will also print water bottles.

A few of the mugs we make

Put "Mug Press" into a Google search and you'll get anything from $49.95 to $289.00; there is no need to buy expensive mug presses that some places will try to sell you. Some of the less expensive ones work just fine. My mug presses cost about $154.00. I have pressed thousands of mugs with this press and it works just fine. I would, however, purchase a spare heating element in case the one that comes with it burns out. It is supposed to last for at least 1,000 mugs, but you don't want to be in the middle of a run, have something go wrong and have to wait a week for a replacement. I have two presses. When I get a large order, I can operate both of them at the same time, and if one goes bad, the other will finish the job. Most of the time I use one for the 11 oz mugs and one for the 15 oz size mug.

There are many other mug presses on ebay. Chose one that fits your needs and price range.

As I am writing this, I am in the middle of sublimating 100 mugs. I'm going to take you from beginning to end to sublimate some mugs, and again, some signs. Since I'm doing the mugs, let's start there.

These are also called photo-mugs as many people will give you photos to put on the mugs. The designs you place on the mugs are actually **IN** the finish and not **ON** the finish. Most mugs are silk-screened, the printing is on top of the finish, and thereby it can be scratched off or rubbed off, and manufacturers charge by the color and the number of mugs to make, plus they often have a setup charge for each color. You can print full-color mugs with no setup and the design is IN the finish. If you rub your hand across the finish with silkscreen, you can feel a rough finish; with sublimation, you won't feel anything.
(HINT--- You can also charge for a setup!)

Printing out of Your Mug Designs—

This step is very important, so pay close attention. Designing and printing out your images for mugs is a very important step, for if you do it right, you won't have to measure anything to get your images placed right on your mugs and they will go on straight. You will have a pattern you can use for all your different images, saving you tons of time and lost mugs. You will ruin many mugs (like I did at the beginning as I didn't have an instructor) if you don't follow these steps closely. I've done a lot of work for you here that you won't have to duplicate later and ruin a lot of mugs in the process.

Most mugs are either 11 oz or 15 oz. You will usually have either a front image or a front and back image.

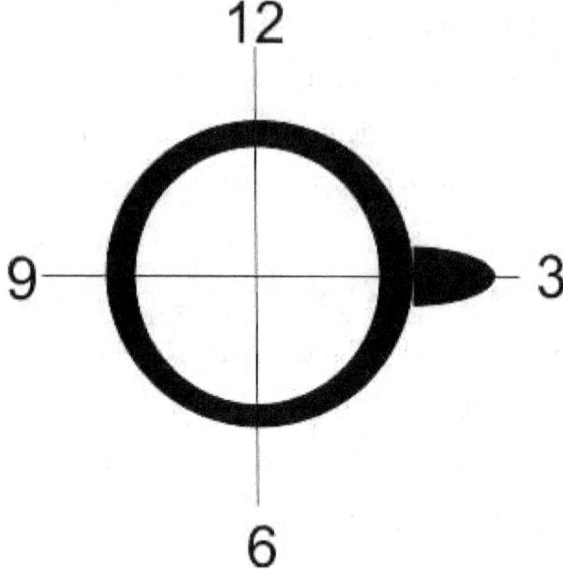

11 oz. Mugs:

The 11 oz mugs are 3.75" high by 10.25" around. The center of the front image (if you look down on the top of a mug, if the handle is at 3 o'clock, the 6 o'clock position is the center of the front of the mug.) The front of the mug is 2-9/16" from the center of the handle. However, our special paper that the image is printed on will go from the side of the handle. Since the handle is approximately ½" wide, we'll subtract half of that to get the center of the front from the side of the handle. Our final computation makes the center of the front image 2-5/16" from the handle. This will be important when we figure where to place our images on our printout.

Don't try to place an image close against the handle. It won't work in the press. Try to keep your images ½" from the handle at a minimum. The heating element isn't as hot at the edges and your image won't transfer completely.

The following image (IMAGE #1) is an actual replica of an 8.5" x 11" printout I use.

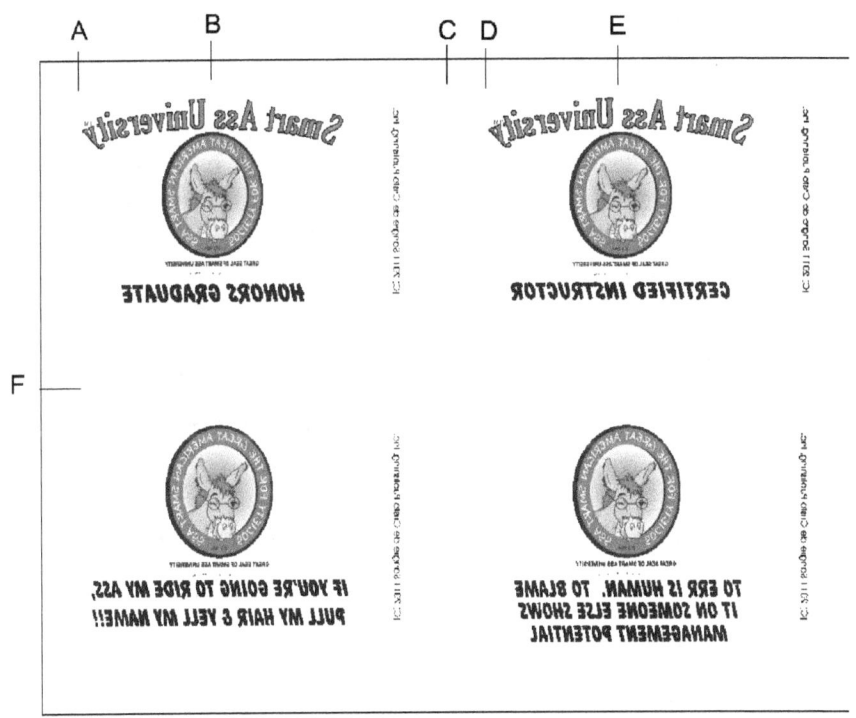

IMAGE #1

This represents the printout for four different mugs. Notice the images are reversed.

A.= ½" from edge gives ½" from the mug handle when placed on mug

B.- Center of image. 2-5/16" from handle or left edge of paper.

C.- This is the half-page (5-1/2") from paper edge and is your cut line. This will also be the edge of the paper for the images on the right above that will go against the handle of the mug.

D.- Same as "A" for the images on the right above after cutting paper in half.

E.- Same as "B" for the images on the right above after cutting paper in half.

F.- Cut line, which is at 4-1/4" from the top of paper. When placing the images on the bottom half of the sheet above, make sure the center of the images are half-way from the 4-1/4" mark to the bottom. Make sure the two upper images are half-way between the top of the page to the 4-1/4" mark ("F").

 I print out four images per sheet. I will cut the page in half at "C" (5.5") and then again at "F" (4.25"). This will give me four image sheets that are 5.5" x 4.25". The center of each image after cutting ("B" & "E") will be 2-5/16" from the handle, so when I place the edge of the paper against the handle, the image will be centered in the front of the mug, and the images will start ½" from the handle ("A"& "D"). This is for RIGHT-HANDED mugs. If you are making left-handed mugs, the 2-5/16" must be from the right of this page. I have kept my images approximately ½" from the top, but try to center them from top to bottom. When you tape the paper to the mug, if you keep the top of the paper at, and even, with the top of the mug, you will have a level image transferred and it will be centered. This may sound difficult, but after you do it a couple times it is very easy and very fast. Don't try to level an image any other way. You will screw up more often than you think and no one wants a crooked image. Use the top of the mug with the top of the paper and you will have a consistently even image every time.

The height of the mug is about 3 7/8" high, so the center of the mug from top to bottom will be about 1-15/16" from the top of the mug and should be from the top of your imaged paper.

Set your images up in reverse as you fill in the images for each mug. If you reverse the page after setting everything up, everything may be off.

11 oz – Double Sided Mugs:
(See IMAGE #2)
To place images on both sides of the mug, follow the directions above for the front of the mug ("A"). The back of

the mug should be centered at 7-7/16" ("B") from the handle. Cut the paper in half at 4¼" ("C") to give your two separate images. Make sure the spacing for the images on the bottom of the page (spacing from the 4 ¼" mark to the top of the image) are the same as the top (from the top edge of the paper to the top of the image.) Again, this is for a right-handed mug, reverse for a left-handed.

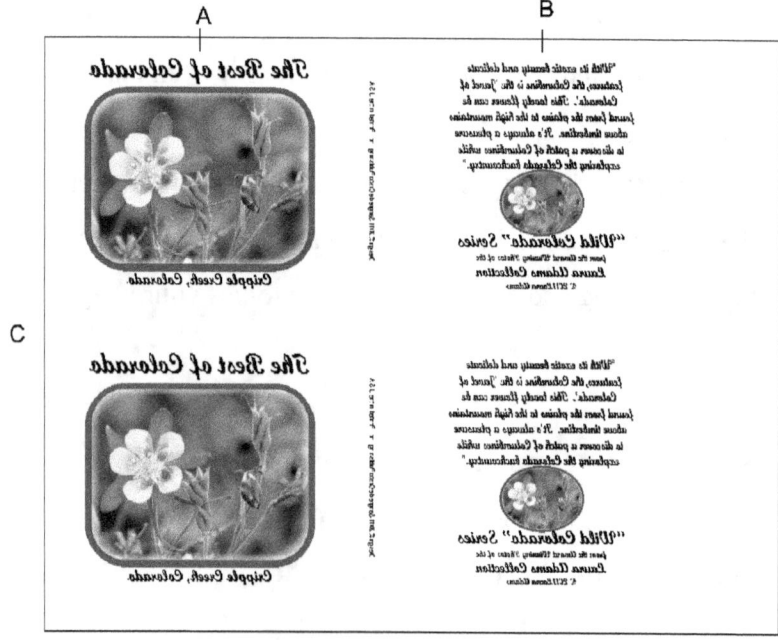

IMAGE #2

This represents the printout of two different mugs on two sides of the mugs.

Pressing Your Mugs:

I always preheat my mug press with a blank mug in it. This helps the mug press heat more evenly. (*Don't use a mug with an image on it as the image will transfer to your heat pad.*)

Sublimation ink turns to a gas when it is heated and **it will also transfer through the sublimation paper to the surface of the heat pad.** To eliminate the inks transferring to the heat pad, cut some standard bond copy paper into strips 9.5" long by 4 ½". Place the sublimation paper containing your image against the handle and even with the top and tape your image to the mug. Place the bond paper loosely over that; it doesn't have to be taped. Place it in the pre-heated mug press, making sure it is snug, but not real tight. If you are pressing a one-sided mug, place the mug so the image is to the rear and the handle is up against the heating element. This will get you the best results if you have a large image or your image is about a ½" away from the handle. This way the mug will move with the closing handle. If you place the handle against the front and the setting is too tight, you will break the handle off the mug. I've done this several times until I learned to place it against the rear part of the clamp.

Pressing a two-sided image: (Make sure the special paper with the image to be transferred is on the mug tight with no play in it!)

If the images are small (At least an inch or so away from the handle, front & back) place the mug in the press with the handle centered in the opening. If the images are large, I suggest placing the mug in the press with the handle against one side of the heating element. Start your press as per the directions of the press. When it is finished, open the press, but keep the mug in and move it so the handle is against the opposite side of the heating element. Close the press and start the press again. This insures the images will get a full heating and the edges won't be feathered. The extra time in the press won't bother the images.

IMPORTANT!!!!!—As soon as you remove the mug from the press, remove the bond paper, then remove the imaged paper by un-taping one side and removing the paper. Be careful not to let the imaged paper move on the mug or come back in contact with the mug as it will still transfer gaseous ink. As soon as the paper has been removed, ***immediately*** place it in some water, preferably room-temperature or warmer. This stops the sublimation process.

If you don't do this, the ink that is on the mug will continue to turn to a gas and you may end up with a ghost-like image. (You will hear crackling when you place the mug into the water. This is normal. It sounds like the mug will crack or break, but I haven't had one do that yet! I have used cold water, but I try to keep it room temp to start.)

---***Don't*** move the mug once it is in the press unless you have to, as even a micro movement of the attached paper image can cause a ghost image.

---***Don't*** re-use the bond paper that you double-wrapped the mug with. Even if you can't see it, it will contain some sublimation ink that was transferred from the gases. Sooner or later, these excess gases will transfer back to the new mug and you will see another image you didn't expect. A wasted mug cost more than a half-ream of bond paper, so it doesn't make sense to test it.

--***Don't*** peel the sublimation paper off the mug. Un-tape one side and take it off that way. Peeling can let parts of the paper move while still on the mug and cause an ink transfer you don't want.

You should have a great looking mug if you follow all these directions!!

15 oz Mugs:

(SEE IMAGE #3)

The 15 oz mugs are 4.625" (4 5/8") high by 10.625" (10 5/8") around. The center of the front image ("A" on the image below) is 2-5/8" from the center of the handle. However, our image that is printed on our special paper will go from the side of the handle. Since the handle is approximately ½" wide, we'll subtract half of that to get the center of the front from the side of the handle. Our final computation makes the center of the front image about 2 3/8" from the handle. This will be important when we figure where to place our images on our printout.

Again, don't try to place an image up against the handle. Try to keep your images ½" from the handle, at a minimum, 3/8".

If you have an image that will also be printed on the back of the cup, the center of that image will be approximately at 8" ("B" on the image below) from the front handle where we started.

Adjust your images up or down on your layout to suit your taste, but try to keep them pretty much centered vertically on the cup.

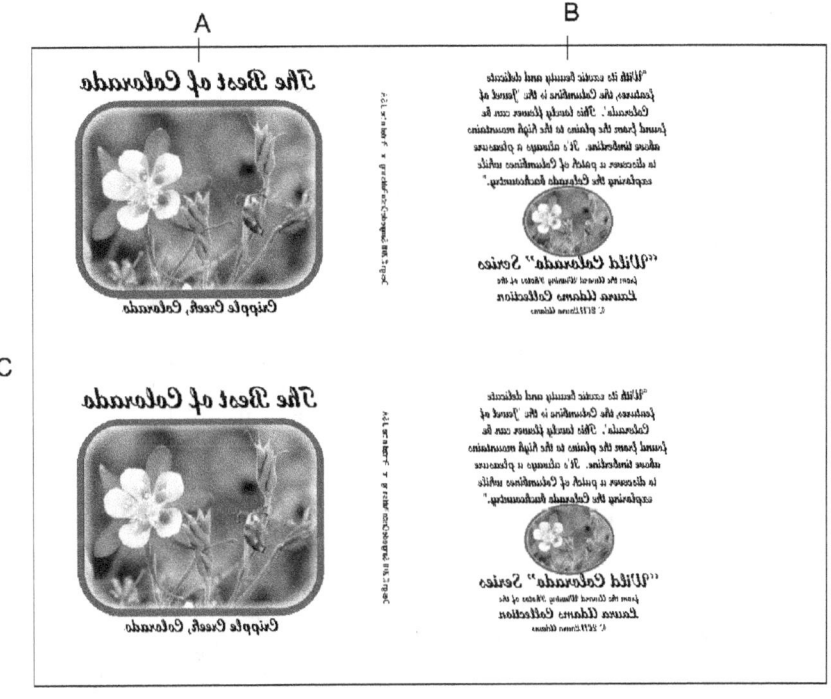

IMAGE #3

Magnets & Signs: Custom signs & magnets can be a real money-maker. The hardboard signs have a high gloss finish and really look nice. When your customers see your samples, they tend to be an easy selling item. You can purchase many different sizes of signs. I use mostly white gloss hardboard tiles as they give great results and the colors are vivid. You can drill small holes in the corners and string a wire hanger or use double stick tape to hang them. Many businesses use magnets and they are available in hardboard or aluminum in several sizes.

You can sublimate any number of different substrates for signs; most are hardboard, aluminum and ceramic. Each has their own properties and times for heating. I usually heat my hardboard for 75 seconds, the aluminum for 75 seconds, and the ceramic for about 7 minutes, all at 400 degrees. You can get magnets in a couple different sizes, but most will be 2" x 3".

I get my signs here:

https://www.coastalbusiness.com/catalogsearch/result/index/?p=3&q=hardboard+sublimation

They are classified as hardboard sublimation photo tiles. There are others with different shapes and sizes.

I get my magnets here:

https://www.coastalbusiness.com/catalogsearch/result/?q=magnets

The magnets come as hardboard, aluminum, plastic and ceramic. They come square, rectangle, heart shape and round.

IMPORTANT!!--- **Many signs (most hardboard & aluminum) come with a peel-off plastic coating on them. Make sure you remove this coating!!!**

Hardboard/Aluminum—Your printouts should be slightly larger than what you are transferring. Try to make it about ¼" larger on the width and height, as this will give you 1/8" on each side. This is important when you need to center your sign or photo onto the substrate. You will really notice it if it is off, especially if you have a border around your work. Off just a little and you will notice it in the final product. Make sure it is perfectly centered and tape it down well. If you need to make your printout the exact size of your sign/magnet, print a square/rectangle line about an 1/8" from around the image, **(SEE IMAGE #4)** but make sure all sides are exactly the same distance away from the image so it will center properly.

IMAGE #4

You can either tape the substrate to your printout (**which is printed out in reverse!**) or use the adhesive spray (just a little). I find the tape easier to use as it allows you to adjust and center your piece. If you aren't perfect with the spray you have to keep pulling it off and readjusting it. I always spray the sheet of magnet impressions as they are small and hard to tape.

PRESSING YOUR SIGN--

Place a large piece of plain paper down on the base of the press, place your sign (with the image adhered) on the paper face up, and then place another piece of large paper down over the sign. If you don't have a large piece of paper, use one or two pieces of bond. We are doing this to protect your press from the excess gasses from the sublimation inks that will come off the printed paper. We don't want the gases adhering to the top or bottom of the press, as they will show up the next time you press a shirt!

Using a medium pressure, close the press. When it is done, remove the printed paper off the sign substrate immediately. Use a pair of gloves if you have to as the substrate will be 400 degrees. Lie the product flat, face up to cool as the gasses are still active and can leave a ghost image.

Ceramic & Glass Tiles: Ceramic and glass tiles can be a beautiful addition to any room. You can frame them, use them as magnets, as a mural, or use them individually. You can create stunning works of art. Tile murals are huge profit makers! I love photos on ceramic. They are beautiful, a great moneymaker, but a little harder to make than mugs. You will probably have to experiment a little with a few before you get it just right. Don't try to take shortcuts, as it will usually end up getting thrown away.

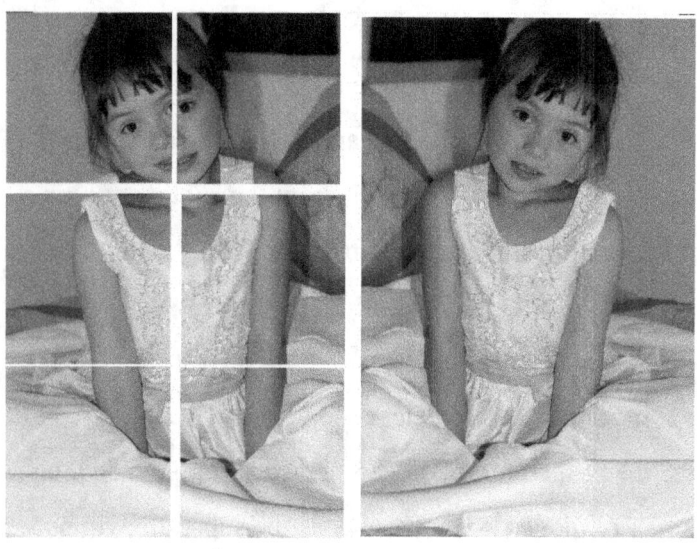

There are many different types of ceramic tiles you can purchase. It's important that you read the times and temperature for each different tile when you purchase the tiles. Every wholesaler that sells these will have the information available for you.

For single tile printouts do your printouts as above, center and tape or spray as described above. For multiple tile printouts, you will need a program that is for that purpose. Corel will do this nicely, but it is expensive. If you can't find a program or someone to do this for you, let me know and I'll see if I can do it for you. The different tile sections have to overlap a slight bit to make up for the curved edges of the tiles.

You will need a Nomex felt pad and a green rubber heat-conductive pad for this operation. The Nomex felt pad is needed in order to make sure the edges of the tiles, which are curved, also get a full sublimation. The green rubber heat-conductive pad is to make sure the tile is evenly heated, as you will be heating the BACK of the tile (the tile is heated face-down and there are ridges that are on most tiles.)

You can get the Nomex felt pad here for about $49.95:
https://www.coastalbusiness.com/high-temperature-nomex-felt-pad-16-x-20-x-05-nmx1620-s.html
You can get the green rubber heat-conductive pad here for about $39.95:

https://www.coastalbusiness.com/sublimation-heating-pad-for-hard-surfaces-wrap1822-s.htmlThere are many different sizes, but these should take care of the majority of your needs. Get larger ones if you think you will need them.

I get my tiles from here as they are heavy and if you purchase at least a $150.00 of merchandise, the freight is free:

https://www.coastalbusiness.com/

This is one item I suggest using the spray adhesive on. Use it very lightly, just a touch will do. Center your tile on the image making sure the image is slightly larger than the tile. Place the Nomex pad on the base of your press. Place a larger sheet of protective paper on top of the pad. Place the tile with the image face down on the protective paper. Place another piece of protective paper on the tile. Place the green heat-conductive pad on top of the paper. Close the press using enough pressure that will force the tile into the Nomex pad. This will insure the tile gets sublimated in the curved edges of the tile. Don't use excessive force as the tile may break.

Most 4" x 4" tiles will need at least eight minutes of time. Make sure you use at least the recommended time, but using more will not hurt it. I have found using a little extra time gives the best results. Larger tiles will need more time and heating more than one tile at a time will need more time.

After the tile has cooled, if you can feel or see a residue on it from the spray, use some Goo-Gone or something like it to remove the residue.

When you remove the tile from the press, be sure to wear a pair of heat-proof gloves as the tile will be 400 degrees and you must remove the paper from it immediately. Don't stand it up, lay it flat with the sublimated side up or you will get ghost impressions on it.

Designs for Your Sublimation

You don't have to be an expert at computer design. I have used www.fiverr.com many times to get something done that I didn't know how to do. It is only $5 and some of the designers on there are really good. If you find one that really knows their stuff, stick with him/her and throw a little extra to them once in awhile and they will do wonders for you. I had a logo that was just two colors and basically just a line art. I asked one designer to color it and make it more three-dimensional. He did a great job and

I gave him an extra $10. He was happy and I got something I would have had to pay hundreds for if I hired someone out of the phone book.

The left one is what I gave him to work with, the right one is what I got for just $5!! I was a great deal!

I had the following logo done for a cookie store. I told them what I wanted and she came up with the following. She charged me $20. I thought it was a real bargain.

Always make sure you have the rights to any photo or logo or design you intend to use. There are many copyrighted label designs out there for sale, so make sure you get the rights to use any design forever.

That's going to be it for now. I have many more items to sublimate, but I want to get this out to everyone. Don't be afraid to experiment; don't be afraid to make mistakes; that's how we learn.

If you have any questions about what I have discussed here, please email me at MainStreetColorado@gmail.com and I'll be glad to help you with whatever I can!

If you're ever in Colorado, stop by Cripple Creek and say HI! We are at "The Hitchin' Post" next door to City Hall and would love to swap stories!

Good Luck, God Bless, and may everyone have HOT PROFITS!!!
Tim Braun
09/13—07/16